ANIMALS IN ART

Louisa Somerville

A Cherrytree book

Designed and reproduced by Touchstone Publishing Ltd

Copyright this edition © Evans Brothers Ltd 2003
Published by Cherrytree Press Ltd, a division of Evans Brothers
2A Portman Mansions
Chiltern St
London WIU 6NR

First published in 1994
First paperback edition published 2003

Designer: David Armitage
Cover designer: Simon Borrough

Cover picture: *Horse Attacked by a Jaguar*, Henri Rousseau

British Library Cataloguing in Publication Data
Sommerville, Louisa
        Animals in Art. – (In Art Series)
        I. Title II. Series
        707

        ISBN 1 84234 181 2

Printed in China through Colorcraft Ltd., Hong Kong

Contents

In every chapter of this book you will find a number of coloured panels. Each one has a symbol at the top to tell you what type of panel it is.

Activity panel Ideas for projects that will give you an insight into the techniques of the artists in this book. Try your hand at painting, sculpting and crafts.

Information panel Detailed explanations of particular aspects of the text, or in-depth information on an artist or work of art.

Look and See panel Suggestions for some close observation, using this book, the library, art galleries, and the art and architecture in your area.

1 Sharing the earth

Imagine a world without animals! No snakes in the rain forest, no lions stalking the African plains, no birds gliding over the mountains and no pets to greet you when you get home. The variety of animals sharing our planet is vast. Add to this the many different techniques and materials that artists have used to depict the animal kingdom throughout history, and we have a treasure trove of works of art from every corner of the globe.

◄ *The bison in this ancient cave painting is wounded, possibly by a hunter. Its legs give way and its head is lowered, as if in pain. Why paint this picture in a remote cave, difficult to reach? Perhaps because the artist believed that being inside the earth would bring him closer to nature.*
[Cave painting of a bison, Altamira, Spain]

Making their mark

Cave paintings have lasted for thousands of years. How can this be when these people had so few materials: no paint as we know it and no brushes? What did they use?

The first paint was made with earth, soot from the fire, charcoal or chalk, mixed with sap, spit or melted animal fat. The first 'brushes' were split sticks, pads of animal fur or fingers;

tools which many artists still use. Shape and form were given to the images by the contours of the rocks.

The paintings have lasted so long because they have been hidden underground, protected from the light and the weather. Only recently discovered, they now have to be protected or they will disappear.

The human connection

The images in this chapter are diverse, but they all demonstrate the close connection between human beings and the rest of the animal kingdom.

Our relationship with animals tends to be based on necessity, fear, love or awe. For thousands of years we have hunted and eaten them, used them as beasts of burden, treasured them as companions, even worshipped them as gods. And, ever since the first artists discovered how to draw with wet earth, we have made images of them.

Perhaps these ancient cave paintings were part of a ritual to make spears fly

▶ *This picture tells a story (see pages 6 and 7). Can you see the animals involved? The beaver and the mink appear twice – in the canoe and in the swirling salmon pattern hanging in the sky above them. The picture has a moody, mysterious feeling. You can almost hear the oars in the black water as the beaver and the mink slip quietly away upriver at night.* [Beaver and the Mink, Susan A. Point]

straight, or to increase the number of animals to hunt. Or maybe the artists believed animals had supernatural powers. Whatever the reason, these paintings are works of considerable skill.

Links with the past

Since early times, people have told stories to make sense of the world around them. The mystery and power of animals have made them a crucial part of these myths. Some are about imaginary beasts.

Think of the Egyptian Sphinx, or a unicorn, or Pegasus, the winged horse from Greek mythology.

Other stories are about real animals. The picture on page 5 is by Susan A. Point, a living Salish artist. (The Salish are an indigenous people from the north-west coast of America.) In her prints, the artist echoes the legends and traditional images of her people. This one depicts the story of the origins of the salmon, an important food

▲ *A race for riderless horses, once an annual event in Rome, was exciting and dangerous. Géricault shows how these untamed horses are seemingly more powerful than the men trying to control them. How has the artist given his picture a sense of drama?* [*Study for* The Race of the Barbarian Horses, *Théodore Géricault*]

6

and therefore much revered. The story goes that a beaver and a mink stole a baby from the salmon-people, fled up-river in a canoe and put the baby in the water. The salmon-people followed, found the baby and from then on lived in the water. They became salmon. Myths connecting the human and animal worlds in this way are common.

Many of the animal images in this book are not realistic. Make a list of them and discuss with friends what is not real about them. Is it the colour, the shape, or has the artist invented a creature from his or her imagination? Or is it because the animal is behaving in an unnatural way or like a human being?

Capturing a likeness

Feelings about animals run deep. If you have pets of your own, you will know how fond of animals people can be. Some artists use a style that emphasizes the emotional appeal of animals and their almost human expressions. Others take a more scientific approach. Whatever the artist's viewpoint, however, it is not easy to capture a likeness. Animals are shy, and not interested in posing for an artist. Even when anatomical studies began in the 15th century and artists such as Leonardo da Vinci dissected animals in their studios in an attempt to portray them correctly (see page 33), accuracy was still very difficult to achieve.

Some artists drew hundreds of sketches before they felt ready to paint a finished picture of an animal. The French artist Géricault, for instance, made a special study of horses, whom he believed had supernatural power. The picture on page 6 is an oil-sketch for a painting he never completed.

The modern approach

Twentieth-century artists know about the anatomy of animals, but some still make images that are imaginative rather than realistic. These may be simply amusing, or they may ask questions about civilization and society. And these days there is a huge choice of materials available.

Is there, for example, a creature living inside an old washing machine, waiting to be released by the touch of a creative imagination? Pablo Picasso enjoyed using waste materials in his sculptures. And the contemporary sculptor, Bill Woodrow, sees a charming water bird in an old frying pan (below).

Animals have been a constant source of inspiration to artists everywhere. By studying these artists' work, we can learn not only about art, but also about religion, science and society.

▼ *This appealing creature is made from an old frying pan. Is it important to know that to appreciate the sculpture? The bird seems to be very much alive, running and turning its head. The marks made by the flame of the stove appear as speckled plumage. The artist has linked nature, reality and imagination. Can you describe how this sculpture has a link with the human world?*
[Water bird, Bill Woodrow]

Monoprint menagerie

Susan A. Point's print on page 5 tells part of the story of the beaver and the mink. You can make a picture that tells a story by making a kind of print, called a monoprint. 'Mono' means one. You take only one print from each image.

What you need
- piece of glass with smooth edges
- piece of thick paper or card the same size or a little larger than the glass
- paints – oil, acrylic, watercolours or water-based printing inks straight from the tube

What you do
1 Choose an animal from a well-known story. Paint your chosen animal on to the glass. Make the paint nice and thick. Start with a simple image, but use as many colours as you like.
2 Place the card on top of your picture and press firmly all over.
3 When you are sure that the whole image is transferred to your paper, peel it off. Your print will now be revealed in reverse.
4 Make alterations and additions directly on to the print while it is still wet. Add texture with the back of a pencil, a sponge or a brush. When you have had some practice, you can fill in your outlines and paint a background before printing.
5 When you try again, experiment by moving the paper gently while printing, to make a slightly blurred image with strange jungle shapes within it.

Human beings first began to share their homes with animals because animals were useful to them. They were a source of food. They worked in the fields. They hunted or chased away pests.

Certain animals became pets, of little use except as friends to human beings. Inevitably, pets became good friends of the family, and because of this owners often had their pets' portraits painted.

Prize animals

Some pets are looked after particularly well. They are entered for competitions that are taken very seriously by their owners. This was as true 200 years ago as it is today. In the 18th century, artists specializing in painting animals travelled the countryside to paint the competition prize-winners with their medals and certificates. These artists were self-taught and their paintings

▲ *You cannot mistake the star of this painting. Spruced up and sparkling for a competition, the Old Spot Pig is enormous – quite out of proportion to her surroundings and admirers. In the background is the village pub where her exploits are doubtless the topic of conversation among the locals. She is a pig to be reckoned with.* [Gloucester Old Spot Pig, *anon*]

are known as 'naïve'. These naïve pictures look flat, with figures like cardboard cut-outs, but the artists certainly knew how to bring out the prize-winning characteristics of the animals – huge size, shiny coats and pricked-up ears. Sometimes the artist included the owner or the keeper in the picture.

A sentimental eye

During the 19th century, paintings in which the artist gave animals human characteristics became immensely popular. The English artist, Sir Edwin Landseer, was famous for such paintings. He started his career painting accurate animal portraits but found he could make a better living by giving his animals almost human expressions. The titles of his paintings tended to emphasize the 'human' emotions of the animals. For example, a picture of a pair of dogs is entitled *Dignity and Impudence*. The tendency to give animals human characteristics can also be

▼ *You can go too far in spoiling your pet! Even 400 years ago, one artist certainly thought so. Loving detail in the costume and the little silver porringer of gruel show that these people are not poor – they have 'more money than sense'.*
[Feeding time, *anon*]

Going too far?

Caricature is a way of making fun of silly behaviour and has always been a popular way of making a point. It may be a political point, or a moral point. In caricature portraits, expressions, facial features and activities are exaggerated, and sometimes make the person concerned look quite unpleasant. Newspaper cartoons of political or well-known people are often caricatures. This painting is not a political caricature, but is making fun of people who spoil their pets. It was painted in the 16th century, but many pet owners today might find a lesson here!

seen in many children's books, such as those of Beatrix Potter (page 26).

Animals, friendship and art

Some people become so fond of their pets that it is said they grow to look like them. Gustave Caillebotte, a 19th-century French artist, must have thought Richard Gallo looked like his poodle, Dick (opposite). Caillebotte was a supporter of Impressionist painters such as Monet and Renoir. He bought their pictures and also adopted their ideas for his own work. The Impressionists were particularly interested in colour and tone and the way light plays on an object to give it form. They liked to work with many small brushstrokes rather than paint large areas of one colour.

Naïve art

Artists who have taught themselves to paint are sometimes called naïve – or unsophisticated. These artists, whose names we often don't know, show the everyday life of ordinary people. They often ignore artistic rules such as perspective – the technique of making objects in the background smaller so they seem further away. They may not paint their figures and objects in the correct proportion to each other. Nevertheless their paintings are often colourful and lively and tell us a good deal about times past. There are several examples of naïve art in this book. Compare the painting of the *Gloucester Old Spot Pig* with those by Hicks (page 38) and Rousseau (page 42).

◀ *Landseer skilfully portrays the sadness of the dog whose master has died. The way the dog so desperately presses itself to the coffin conveys its dejection at the loss of its best friend.*
[The Old Shepherd's Chief Mourner, *Sir Edwin Landseer*]

▲ The subdued colours
of the background
concentrate your eye on
the likenesses between
the two jaunty figures in
this picture. How has the
artist made them look
alike? Most of the lines
in the painting are
horizontal or vertical.
Can you see one
important diagonal line
that gives life to the
picture and accentuates
the similarities between
dog and man?
[Richard Gallo and his
Dog Dick, Gustave
Caillebotte]

Exotic aristocrats

While domestic animals
remained a popular subject
for paintings, some artists
found employment painting
the portraits of exotic species
of animals brought back from
newly discovered parts of the
world. Jacques-Laurent
Agasse was an early 19th-
century Swiss painter who
worked in England for most
of his career. Like the
anonymous artist of the
Gloucester Old Spot Pig

(page 10), he specialized in
animal portraits, but he was a
trained artist and much more
fashionable and expensive.

The giraffe in Agasse's
painting (page 14) must have
been an incredible sight to
people who had never before
seen such a creature. It was a
present to the British king,
George IV, from Mohammed
Ali, Viceroy of Egypt. It came
to England with its keeper
and the keeper's servant to
look after it. The poor creature

▼ *The cows in the background don't seem to mind the fuss being made of the elegant, sensitive creature sharing their field. The giraffe's markings, mane and tufted horns are shown in minute detail. Do you think this picture is a straightforward record of a scene – or is it a sentimental portrait?*
[The Nubian Giraffe, *Jacques-Laurent Agasse*]

Look alike

Do you have a friend who looks like his or her pet? What is alike about them? Look at the head to begin with. Is the owner's hair the same colour or texture as the pet's fur? Do they have the same shaped head? Are their eyes alike? What about their mouths or ears? Can you capture an expression they both have sometimes – mischievous or cross perhaps? You may need to exaggerate their similarities, just as Caillebotte did.

What you need
• pencil, paint or crayons
• paper
• a friend to sit for you with his or her pet, or a photograph of them to work from

What you do
Make a picture of your friend with the animal. Concentrate on their expression, the lines of their bodies, the way they hold their heads. Connect them by some action – going for a walk like Richard Gallo and Dick, or sitting in a chair together. You could make your portrait a bit sentimental by giving owner and pet matching bows or collars, or you could draw a caricature like the one shown here.

had a difficult journey, and survived only one English winter.

The viceroy also sent a giraffe to Charles X, king of France. This animal fared rather better, surviving both the voyage by sea and the month-long journey from Marseilles to Paris on foot. During the journey, it was protected from the rain by a special mackintosh cape and accompanied by three cows to provide the 25 litres of milk per day it required. From its neck hung the Koran, Islam's holy book. The giraffe lived in the botanical gardens in Paris for a grand 20 years.

3 Animals at work

It is difficult for us to imagine how important animals once were in everyday life. Before the days of machines and synthetic materials, they provided not only food, but warmth, clothing and transport. They often worked hard, in poor conditions and were sometimes mistreated. In many countries of the world today, this is still the case.

Ever since animals were first farmed thousands of years ago, artists have portrayed them at work. Sheep and goats were the first animals to be domesticated, followed by cattle and poultry. All of these animals can be seen in the art and sculpture of ancient civilizations. But artists throughout history have often chosen to ignore the hardship and the dirt, showing animals at work as happy and 'squeaky clean'. This is due in part, as we have seen in the preceding chapters, to the genuine affection people feel towards the animals that share their lives.

Around the world, the different animals used for transport are reflected in art. So, for example, while images of the horse dominate European art, the camel features in Middle Eastern paintings and the elephant in Indian art.

Village life

In southern Mesopotamia (modern-day Iraq) 700 years ago, people travelled by camel. In those days, stories were illustrated by hand. These paintings were beautifully designed and highly decorated with rich colours and detailed pattern. Swirling shapes were made by drawing a feather over lines of wet paint, a technique used by the artist in the lively picture opposite. The painting not only tells a story but shows us what village life was like in Mesopotamia at that time.

Art for everyone

More than 500 years later, in 19th-century America, people were still dependent on animals for many daily tasks. The picture on page 18, by the printmakers Currier & Ives, shows a horse-drawn fire engine rushing to the scene of a fire in New York City. Currier & Ives used a fast new printing process to make prints for people who could not afford paintings. Speed was vital if such newsworthy pictures were to sell. People had to see the pictures before

Find other images of animals at work, in farming for instance, or in war. How have the artists portrayed them? Do they seem contented, or are they thin, frightened or exhausted. Do you think the images are true to life or idealized? How can you tell?

▶ *The artist has captured the camels' almost human, supercilious expressions perfectly. What other animals does he depict? Where do they live? Which were used as a source of food and which for clothing – or both?*
[Abou Zayd and Al-Harith questioning villagers, *from the Assemblies of al-Hariri*]

their interest was captured by some other thrilling event.

The printing process used by Currier & Ives is called lithography, a process based on the principle that grease and water do not mix. A picture is drawn on a stone (nowadays zinc or aluminium is normally used) with a greasy crayon. The stone is wetted and oily ink rolled over it. The ink sticks only to the greasy drawing. A print is taken from the stone using damp paper.

Circus tricks

Although most work done by animals is useful to us, no such claim can be made for the tricks animals perform at a circus. Ever since ancient Greek times, animals have been put to work to entertain people. Two thousand years ago, Julius Caesar built an amphitheatre in Rome used for chariot races and the spectacle of Christians being fed to hungry lions. Over the years, animal performances became a regular feature of circuses.

During the 19th century, circus shows, including acrobats and clowns, became very popular. The brilliant colours and the dramatic poses of both humans and

▼ *We can almost hear the frightened neighing of horses, the pounding of hooves, the crackle of flames. The depiction of heroism, speed and excitement may seem effortlessly achieved, but it took 12 women to colour a print like this by hand, using green, red and yellow paint. It had to be printed quickly and distributed while the fire was still news.*
[The Life of a Fireman: The Metropolitan System, *Currier & Ives*]

animals made the circus an appealing subject for artists. However, by the end of the century some painters recognized that the animals were often treated with cruelty and indignity.

In the 1920s, the British painter Clifford Hall enjoyed the glamour and excitement of the circus, but at the same time his painting above portrays the animals as caged beasts that are denied their freedom.

Colour crazy

By the end of the 19th century, developments in photography meant that artists were no longer needed to record events. They experimented with new ways of using shape and colour rather than reproducing what they saw. A group of German painters used colours to represent different emotions. They called themselves *Der Blaue Reiter* (The Blue Rider) after the title of a picture by one of the group.

19

Colours with meaning

Franz Marc wrote about his ideas on colour. He believed that blue could be identified as male – which he interpreted as sharp and spiritual. Yellow he saw as female – soft, cheerful and sensual. Red represented the material, brutal and heavy. According to his theory, if you mixed spiritual blue with brutal red, the resulting purple would be unbearably sad and would need feminine yellow to uplift it. If you mixed yellow and red into a blazing orange, the sharpness of blue would calm it down.

One of these artists, Franz Marc, specialized in images of animals – his best known paintings are those of a blue horse. Marc was not appreciated in his own time. His painting above does not portray the cow as a working animal, provider of milk. Instead, it expresses Marc's impression of the cow as a joyful creature.

Imagine how shocking his yellow cow would have looked to people who were only used to seeing accurate images of animals.

▲ *Franz Marc shows us a buttercup-yellow cow, jumping crazily through the air, mooing with joy. He chooses red for the field and blue for the mountains beyond. Everything is recognizable, but highly stylized. Read the information box on colours with meaning (left). Why do you think Marc has chosen these colours for the painting?*
[Yellow Cow, *Franz Marc*]

Wax picture

Franz Marc used colours to represent different feelings. Here's a way to try out his ideas by making a picture in wax.

What you need
- paper or card with a surface that will accept wax crayon
- wax crayons, coloured and black
- scratching tool – a very small screwdriver or blunt kitchen knife will do

What you do
1 Choose an animal that you associate with a particular emotion, such as joy or sadness. Think of the colour that best expresses that feeling.
2 Cover the paper with wax crayon of your chosen colour. When the paper is thickly covered, cover it again all over with black wax crayon. You will now have two layers of wax.
3 With your scratching tool, trace a faint outline of your chosen animal on to the wax.
4 Go over your faint image, this time digging quite deeply with your scratching tool to reveal the colour beneath the black layer.
5 You will now have a coloured animal peeping through the black surface.
Note Later you can experiment with other colours, but always use a dark colour over a light one.

 # Weird and wonderful

A dragon breathing fire, a creature that is half human, half animal, a woman with serpents instead of hair; these strange beasts could be the terrifying stars of modern science fiction films, but in fact they all have their origins in ancient myths. Myths are stories that are handed down through the generations and become an important part of the history of a culture. Artists enjoy making images of mythical beasts because they can give their imagination full flight. And today some of the most popular stories are about imaginary animals, such as Toad of Toad Hall and Fantastic Mr Fox. Although we know such creatures do not really exist, we still enjoy the stories.

The horse-men of Greece

The myths of ancient Greece include stories about centaurs. These creatures were supposed to have the top half of a man and the legs and torso of a horse. They appeared as warlike, lustful beasts who liked to drink wine, which made them wild and uncontrollable. Fights between centaurs were commonplace and some artists have depicted fierce battles between them. The most famous centaur was Chiron, who was not, however, uncontrollable at all, but a wise, kind creature and teacher of the Greek heroes Jason and Achilles.

Centaurs probably had a basis in fact. In remote regions of ancient Greece there were communities who would catch and tame wild horses. This skill might have seemed superhuman to outsiders, to whom the horse was a new and wonderful animal. People came to think of the magnificent horse and its horseman as one creature. A person who can ride a horse well is still said to be 'at one' with the horse.

Behind the mask

In many cultures animals are supposed to have magic powers, which are evoked in ritual ceremonies of music and dance. Behind an animal mask, the wearer can take on its characteristics and weave its magic. Dance movements imitating those of the animal – a leaping deer or the flight of a bird perhaps – serve to make the magic more effective.

Although there are similarities in the spirit worlds of different cultures, there are many variations, too. For example, the Inuit people of Greenland, Canada and northern Alaska believe that their animal masks, carved

► *This painting tells the story of the triumph of Virtue over Vice. Minerva, the goddess of Wisdom, represents Virtue. Adorned with olive branches as a sign of her virtue, she holds the lance of wisdom in one hand and grips the hair of a centaur, representing Vice, with the other. See how the centaur's face and gesture express his submission to her higher power. Woven on Minerva's dress are interlocking diamond rings, the emblem of Lorenzo de Medici, who paid Botticelli to paint the picture. The painting represents the wisdom in Lorenzo which has overcome the centaur – or beast – in him.*
[Minerva and the Centaur, *Sandro Botticelli*]

from wood, whalebone and walrus tusks, are the homes of spirits. In Africa, masks are often used in rituals about farming the land. In the ceremonies of the Gurunsi, a farming group from the Côte d'Ivoire, West Africa, every mask has a specific dance rhythm attached to it. Each dancer learns the steps for all the different rhythms, enabling him to wear any mask. The aim of the dances is to control an energy in nature, which otherwise might bring evil on the community.

Good or evil?

The dragon is a well-known mythical creature in both western and eastern culture. In Christian art the dragon represents Satan, but in some other cultures it is seen as a force for good. In China, for example, one type of dragon is associated with water and worshipped as the bringer of rain and good harvests. It may be that the idea of this sort of dragon originated in the alligator. Dragons also play an important part in Chinese festivals. During New Year festivities, paper dragons are paraded in the streets to see off the evil spirits of the past year.

The myth of the dragon reached Japan from China around the 6th century, where it retained its significance as a rain spirit. Over the years, four separate dragon images developed

▼ *This wooden bird's-head mask from Africa would have been worn by a performer in a ritual dance. It did not cover the wearer's face but sat on his head like a hat. It must have been heavy to wear. See how skilfully the mask is carved. The carver would have come either from a family of carvers or be apprenticed to such a family. What kind of magic do you think would be made with this mask? [Gurunsi mask]*

▲ *This dramatic picture shows a three-clawed rain dragon and two tigers, symbols of the wind. It was made using the woodcut technique described on page 30. Each colour was printed separately, and enormous skill was needed to achieve all the lines and shading. The larger the block of wood, the harder it is to achieve an even print, which is why this picture was made in three panels.* [Dragon and Two Tigers, *Utagawa Sadahide*]

representing heaven, earth and sea, rain and the underworld.

For hundreds of years, Japan was a closed society with virtually no contact with the outside world. In the 19th century the country began to open its doors. The artist Utagawa Sadahide took advantage of the new freedom and made his living by portraying everything foreign – including animals, such as tigers, that were being brought to Japan for the first time. The tigers in the picture above may be based on ones Sadahide saw, or they may, like the dragon, be the product of his imagination.

Medieval bestiary

In the Middle Ages, pictures of animals could be found in a bestiary – a kind of illustrated dictionary of living creatures. Bestiaries were far from accurate – most of the animals depicted were based on legend and folklore. However, at that time artists were not concerned with drawing animals realistically. It was believed that everything in nature was there to reveal the will of God. Animals in the bestiary were usually symbols of, for example, love, purity, or the devil. Artists painted animals in order to convey these moral messages.

Talking animals

In many children's stories animals are given human characteristics, turning real animals into imaginary beings. Many such tales are about animals that talk, reason, feel emotions and even dress like people. Giving animals these human characteristics is called 'anthropomorphism'. Many artists make a career illustrating well-known stories such as Puss-in-Boots, Brer Rabbit and Winnie-the-Pooh. They can portray human activities and emotions on the faces of animals with great realism.

Some, like Beatrix Potter, write the stories, too. Her books are about animals that are naughty, clever or charming, running their lives, homes and businesses in the same way as humans, with varying degrees of success. The humans in the books are usually shown as a threat to animals, and because of this the animals have to overcome dangers or difficulties.

Look at some illustrated books of animal stories. Do they include images of animals with human characteristics and feelings? How has the artist conveyed them in the portraits of animals? Where else can you find examples of animals behaving like humans? How about television commercials – or think of your favourite cartoon characters.

▼ *The tables are turned! Two mice dressed as humans take their revenge on a cat that has been chasing them. The mice's expressions are animated and full of wicked glee.* [*Illustration from* The Roly-Poly Pudding, *Beatrix Potter*]

Make your own bestiary

The strange creature shown on this 14th-century tile is a mixture of a dodo (now extinct) and a boar, all in one body. The artist must have looked up these creatures in a bestiary and then had fun deciding which bits to put where! You could make your own bestiary and keep it in a scrap book or on index cards.

What you need
- photographs of animals from magazines
- scissors
- glue

What you do
1 Cut round the outline of each animal. Then try swapping bits of the animals around. See how they look with different heads, an extra tail and so on.
2 When you've made up some weird and wonderful beasts, stick them into a scrapbook or on to cards.
3 Invent names for them and write them underneath. You could write a brief description of each beast, such as where it lives and what it eats.

Beatrix Potter spent much of her childhood drawing and painting. Her knowledge of animals came from close observation of her pets, farm animals, wild animals in the fields and woods near her home, and visits to the zoo. Her illustrations are charmingly drawn and have remained popular with both children and adults.

5 ▷ Science and art

▲ *Dürer has engraved wonderfully intricate patterns on his woodcut of a rhinoceros. Some of them are accurate but others are imaginary. Do you think he caught the character of the animal well, even though he never saw it? Some people believed that the rhinoceros was the same animal as the unicorn. Is there anything in Dürer's woodcut that suggests he took this idea seriously?* [Rhinoceros, *Albrecht Dürer*]

During the 14th century in Italy, a new cultural and artistic movement arose, inspired by the art, poetry and stories of the ancient Greeks and Romans. This movement was called the Renaissance, meaning 'rebirth'. Artists began to show the contours and texture of the human form, as they had done in ancient times. At the same time, there was a renewed interest in nature. Artists started to examine animals more closely and to sketch them from life.

The speed at which animals moved made it hard

to study their movements closely. Features or body markings could be seen on dead or sleeping animals, but how, for instance, could you find out how many legs are on the ground at the same time when a horse is galloping? And if you couldn't get close to a shy animal, how could you see the way it rested, ate or mated?

Like the giraffe brought from Egypt and painted by Agasse (page 14), exotic creatures that reached Europe attracted huge curiosity. Sometimes animals were brought back by ship from faraway lands, or travellers brought stories and descriptions of the animals they had seen. The pioneering sailors who set sail from Europe to unexplored parts of the world took artists with them to record the plants and animals they saw.

Animal curiosity

Albrecht Dürer, an early 16th-century German artist, had an insatiable curiosity. He wanted to find out all he could about animals – especially exotic ones. He kept numerous pets and travelled widely to see as many unusual creatures as possible. In 1515 a ship from India

▶ The first kangaroo skin was brought back to Britain from Captain Cook's voyage to Australia aboard the ship Endeavour. *Stubbs was asked to paint it. First it had to be reconstructed. The skin was stuffed and inflated with air to make it lifelike. The result is charming, but, as you can see, not very accurate because Stubbs had never seen a live kangaroo. It looks as if he put some of the stuffing in the wrong place!*
[Kangaroo, *George Stubbs*]

Woodcuts

A woodcut is a kind of print. First, the artist's design is drawn on to a block of wood. Then the cutter uses a knife, similar to a penknife, to carefully cut all the wood away from the sides of the lines that the artist has drawn. Ink is applied to the surface of the block, and the block is then pressed down on to paper.

Dürer's woodcuts marked a major advance in technique. He trained his cutters to reproduce every line of his drawings. This produced much more complicated and sophisticated designs than ever before.

arrived in Lisbon, in Portugal. On board was a rhinoceros, the first to arrive in Europe for over 1000 years, and its fame

quickly spread. However, Dürer never saw the animal. His woodcut of the rhinoceros on page 28 was based on a sketch of the animal sent from Lisbon to accompany a newsletter. Dürer lived in Nüremburg in a street next to the armourers' quarter, and at the time he saw the newspaper sketch was engaged in designing armour. This is probably how he got his inspiration for his woodcut.

Anatomical enquiries

In the 18th century, people became increasingly interested in art as a means of recording the natural world. George Stubbs made a lifetime's study of the

Women abroad

In the past, women like Maria Sybille Merian had to overcome great difficulties to practise their art. Women were expected to stay at home and paint as a hobby, not to compete directly with men. In the 19th century, the French painter Rosa Bonheur, although a successful artist, had to dress as a man in order to enter the horse market in Paris, where she observed the animals at first hand. Try to find out about other women artists who lived in earlier times. What problems did they encounter?

◄ *Three or four colours are enough for Merian to suggest the fantastic, decorative patterns and shapes of two dangerous creatures entwined in combat. Who is eating whom in the picture?* [Alligator and Snake, *Maria Sybille Merian*]

▲ *The delicacy of the bird's rose-coloured plumage and misty landscape contrast with the stylized head of the spoonbill and the plants. How useful do you think it is as a scientific painting? Compare it with Bill Woodrow's* Water bird *on page 8. Which seems more alive?*
[Roseate Spoonbill, John James Audubon]

anatomy (physical structure) of animals in an attempt to depict them accurately (see page 29). Stubbs started his career lecturing in human anatomy to medical students, and his earliest works are illustrations for a textbook of midwifery (all about the birth of babies). Stubbs had only the help of his wife, Mary, to hoist great animal carcasses – mostly horses – into his studio. Here he set up huge vats for boiling down fatty tissue as he uncovered layer after layer of flesh, muscles, organs and bones. His book, *Anatomy of a Horse*, containing accurate drawings of each stage of dissection, is still in use today.

Intrepid traveller

Stubbs was living proof that art and science can go hand in hand, but he was not the first. Nearly 100 years earlier, Maria Sybille Merian had spent two years in Surinam in South America – a remarkably intrepid adventure for a European woman at that time. She patiently observed animals, insects and plants and made detailed watercolour paintings of them. Watercolours are useful for quick, on-the-spot studies. In those days, oil paints were too cumbersome and messy to carry about. It wasn't until the 1840s that oil paints in tubes became available, enabling the Impressionists to paint out of doors with ease.

American adventure

John James Audubon also used watercolour. This American naturalist recorded every known American bird and quadruped (four-footed animal) in a monumental study that took him on some hair-raising adventures across the country, from the mountains to the swamps. Audubon sometimes killed as many as 100 birds in order to paint a likeness of a species, with varying degrees of accuracy. Yet now, his name is given to one of the largest conservation organizations in the USA.

Photography to the rescue

It was not until Eadweard Muybridge found a way to take photographs in quick succession that the riddle of the galloping horse was solved. His first experiments involved placing 20 cameras in a row, and then taking photographs one after the other. Next he invented a camera with a shutter which made his life easier. Ever since, his photographs of moving creatures have been a work of reference and an inspiration for imaginative images.

Until Muybridge's photographs, artists had tended to show galloping horses with outstretched legs, as if they were flying through the air. Now they could see exactly how a horse's legs moved. Horses in paintings never looked the same again.

▼ *This sequence of photographs makes it clear how the horse's legs move when it is jumping. This is one of hundreds of experiments by Muybridge in recording locomotion. In other experiments he studied running, jumping, turning, galloping, leaping. Could you use this sequence for an imaginative painting – a beast with many legs moving at the same time, or a horse moving through the sky, perhaps?*
[Horse and Rider in Motion, *Eadweard Muybridge*]

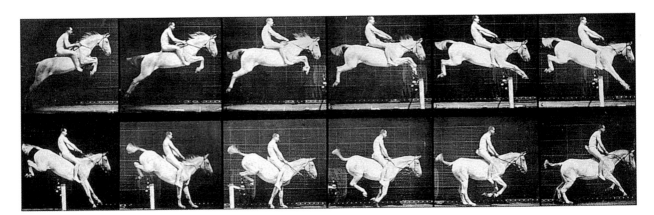

Leonardo's drawings

Leonardo da Vinci was a genius of the Renaissance in Italy. Not only was he one of the greatest artists of all times, painting such masterpieces as the *Mona Lisa*, he was also a gifted sculptor, architect, musician and scientist, making drawings of flying machines, fountain pens, and many other devices which were claimed to have been invented much later.

Like Dürer, Leonardo was a close observer of nature and made studies of both humans and animals, filling his notebooks with hundreds of sketches and detailed drawings. And like Stubbs, he made a scientific study of the anatomy of the horse, fascinated both by its natural beauty and by its wild energy in motion.

▲ *In this study for a painting, Leonardo is more interested in the horses than the riders, who are roughly sketched. The horses, on the other hand, are observed in detail. See how carefully the artist has shown the movement of the animals' legs with light rapid strokes of the pen.*
[Two Horsemen, *Leonardo da Vinci*]

Animal guesses

Dürer based his woodcut of the rhinoceros on a description of the animal. You could try drawing animals in this way with a friend.

What you need
- pictures of animals
- paper, pencils and crayons

What you do
1 Each of you chooses a picture of an animal without showing the other.

2 Take it in turns to describe your animal (without naming it) while the other person makes a drawing according to the description. Is it hard to do? How accurate are your drawings? Which aspect of each animal is hardest to describe? Remember to describe the shape of the animal, its expression and its texture.
Note Another idea is to ask several people to draw the same animal and compare their efforts. You will be amazed at the results!

6 Gods and beasts

Ever since people painted pictures of animals on the walls of caves, human beings have used animals as symbols in their efforts to understand the world around them. Each group of people has its own beliefs with which certain animals are associated. Sometimes people have been so much in awe of animals that they have worshipped them as gods. They prayed to them to provide for their needs and to protect them from all kinds of evil, real and imagined.

Animals are sometimes shown as servants of the gods, or as their friends. It was often thought that only a supernatural being or someone close to a god could tame and understand animals.

World beliefs

In the Hindu religion, animals are mostly seen as the servants of the gods, usually providing transport. For example, in the picture on the opposite page the god Krishna is shown riding the half-human Garuda bird, while the god Indra rides

Why do you think people believed that wild creatures, real or imaginary, could be tamed? Do you know any stories about fearsome creatures from outer space that would be terrifying if they were let loose in the world? Could you make a picture of one, together with the kind of hero or god that might tame them?

an elephant. This picture tells a Hindu myth. Krishna persuaded the people to stop worshipping Indra, god of rain. Indra was furious and sent endless rain on earth. Krishna lifted up a mountain with his finger and turned it red hot so that it dried up the rain as it fell. After a week, Indra gave in and arrived on a white elephant to pay his respects to Krishna.

Some animals in the Hindu faith are associated with gods, such as Ganesh the elephant-headed god and Hanuman the monkey god. In other parts of the world, too, there are animal gods. The people of the north-west coast of North America believe in a trickster god, named Raven. He is a creator of things, but he is also a joker and a cheat.

In the Christian faith,

▶ *The diagonal lines and billowing clouds give a feeling of the pace and energy attributed to the Hindu god Krishna. The humans may look anxious, but the gods sitting serenely in the sky leave no doubt that Krishna will triumph in this battle. Can you see which parts of Garuda are bird and which are human?*
[Krishna in combat with Indra]

animals are used as symbols representing different aspects of humanity. Jesus is associated with the lamb – symbol of innocence and purity – and with the lion, symbol of the Resurrection. The medieval bestiaries (see page 25), in which these symbols were recorded, became an important source of animal symbolism for later artists.

Supernatural power

Some holy people were believed to hold supernatural powers that enabled them to tame wild beasts. St Jerome, for example, took a thorn from a lion's foot, and the lion was so grateful that it became his faithful companion.

The most famous saint with a special relationship

▶ *Molnár emphasizes the gentle nature of St Francis of Assisi by painting a half-circle of little birds listening enraptured as he preaches to them about Jesus. The icy peaks and a frozen lake surrounding St Francis suggest the loneliness of a monk's life. His upraised hands and eyes and his plain brown robe tell of his simplicity. The lily at his feet is a symbol of purity. The painting is enclosed in an arched frame, reminding us of a stained glass church window.*
[St Francis Preaching to the Birds, C. Pál Molnár]

▲ *More than 2000 years old, this colourful image is made from hundreds of small ceramic pieces fitted together to make a mosaic floor. Dionysus, the Greek god of wine, seems quite at home on the back of such a fearsome beast. The leopard wears a necklace of vine leaves and grapes to indicate his subservience to the god.*
[*Mosaic of the god Dionysus riding a leopard*]

Ancient Egypt

The ancient Egyptians observed the creatures around them – crocodiles, jackals, cats and snakes – and believed that gods and goddesses existed in them. They saw these animals as the equals and protectors of the pharaohs. One goddess could change herself into a cat and another had the body of a woman and the ears and horns of a cow. Yet another took the form of a pregnant hippopotamus. The jackal-headed god, Anubis, was keeper of the Underworld. These gods and goddesses appear in paintings on the walls of Egyptian temples and tombs, and as stone statues. The Egyptians did not worship these animals as gods, but saw them as symbols of the gods.

with animals was St Francis, who was born in Assisi, in Italy, in 1182. It was said that animals could understand his words and that once he preached a sermon to the birds. He was supposed to have tamed all wild things, including a wolf that terrorized the neighbourhood. St Francis can be seen in paintings from medieval times to the present day. He is usually shown wearing the dark brown habit of the Franciscan order of friars, which he founded. His habit is secured by a belt with three knots, symbolizing the friars' vows of poverty, chastity and

obedience. The painting of St Francis on page 36 is by a 20th-century Hungarian artist, C. Pál Molnár. Molnár was a book illustrator as well as a painter of religious images.

The ancient Greeks believed in a whole family of gods and goddesses, and animals played an important part in their beliefs. The mosaic of Dionysus (above), Greek god of wine, shows him riding a leopard. Like St Francis, Dionysus had supernatural power over wild creatures.

The flood and the ark

Some stories occur again and again in different religions. Scientists have discovered evidence of a great flood that covered vast areas of the earth, a catastrophe passed down as a legend in many different cultures. Most famous is the story of how the Hebrew god of the Old Testament told Noah to build an ark in which to save one pair of each animal, a male and a female, until the flood waters had gone down and they could populate the earth again. Many artists have used this theme to display their knowledge and skill in animal painting. The idyllic setting allowed them to show off their landscape skills too.

In harmony with God

Edward Hicks, whose version of Noah's ark is on this page, was an early 19th-century American artist. He wanted his art to reflect his belief in a natural harmony between humans, animals and God, all living in a *Peaceable Kingdom* – the title of one of his paintings, of which he made over 100 versions. Like the naïve artists of the 18th century, Hicks had no professional artistic training. The animals in his paintings are primitive and flat looking, but their peaceful facial expressions suggest that they are in harmony with God. As well as being an artist, Hicks was also a Quaker preacher (the Quakers are a Christian sect), and a coach-maker and sign writer.

▼ *Hicks' animals are from many countries, but his Ark is unmistakably a barn from New England, in the USA, resting on a barge. The lamb, symbolizing Jesus, stands next to the lion, suggesting that all creatures, even troublesome human beings, can live together in union with God. Can you find any other unlikely placing of two species next to each other?* [Noah's Ark, *Edward Hicks*]

Animal stencil

Artists have often used animals as symbols in their paintings. Why not adopt your own personal animal symbol? By making a stencil you can print your symbol again and again. Choose your favourite animal or your zodiac sign (if that is an animal). Or find out in which Chinese year you were born and adopt the animal to which the year is dedicated. Or choose an animal that reflects your personality. Are you a wise owl, for example, a cheeky monkey, or a bit of a slippery snake?

What you need
- large sheet of thin card
- pencil and scissors
- cutting board and craft knife
- newspaper
- old toothbrush
- water-based paints
- old plate or similar
- old shirt or overall

What you do
1 Draw the outline of your animal in the middle of the sheet of card. Make the shape fairly simple. You need a large piece of card, but make your drawing quite small. Keep the outline really simple.

2 Put your card on a cutting board. Carefully push the point of the craft knife into the middle of your drawing and cut out the shape. Your stencil is now ready for trying out.

3 Cover your working area with newspaper. It's a good idea to put on an overall or old shirt at this stage.

4 Put some scrap paper under the stencil to try it out. Pour thin paint on to the plate. Dip the toothbrush in the paint. Hold the brush above the stencil and draw the closed blades of the scissors over the bristles towards you. This will splatter the paint away from you on to the stencil.

5 Lift up the card to see the result. Have you used enough paint? Can you tell what animal it is supposed to be? You may need to experiment with more stencils and paint.

6 When you are happy with your results, use your stencil to decorate writing paper, notebooks and so on. You could outline your animal using a gold or silver pen.

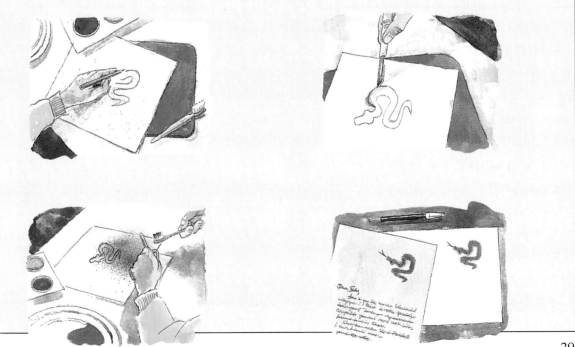

Born free

Animals in the wild are elusive. Their speed and their camouflage protect them from predators, and human beings have a healthy respect for their temper and their teeth! Nevertheless, artists all over the world have constantly risen to the challenge of trying to capture their likeness. Some followed Stubbs' realism. Others drew stylized images of them. This means the animals are recognizable but not realistic. Some of their features are exaggerated or altered to suit our feelings about them.

Art or tool?

In ancient cultures, the close links between plant and animal life (including human beings) were understood. Each needed the other to survive. So even a simple event like making medicine became a magic ritual to harness nature to cure ailments. Because it was magic, the tools used by the medicine-maker were lovingly carved and decorated, often in a stylized fashion. The anteater on the page opposite is an example of this type of carving.

Ways of seeing

Henri Rousseau, a 19th-century French artist, liked to paint exotic subjects – foreign landscapes, ferocious animals, tropical plants and forests – in a simple style. Like the unknown artist of the *Gloucester Old Spot Pig* and the American artist Edward Hicks, Rousseau is sometimes known as a naïve artist because he received no formal training. He was a customs official, who was also a painter. Unlike many of today's wildlife artists, he never experienced the jungle at first hand. He based his tropical plants on those he saw in the botanical gardens in Paris, escaping from the city only in his imagination. His wild animals he often modelled on those he had seen in other painters' work.

Like the carving of the anteater, Rousseau's painting of a savage attack on a horse by a jaguar (page 42) is stylized.

► *This ancient anteater is carved in stone. He sits up in a human-like manner and his main features are exaggerated. We do not know what purpose the carving served. Perhaps the anteater held medicine in his hollow pot-belly. Or he may have been a fertility symbol. He was not meant to be simply a work of art. Maybe he was a tool stylized to show his magic properties in the service of human beings.* [Anteater *from New Guinea*]

Rousseau may have seen paintings by Stubbs and Géricault who had also depicted great cats attacking horses but in a realistic, dramatic style, quite different from his own. See if you can find their images and compare them.

The colours Rousseau used are brilliant and flat, with no modelling. His jungles are all-enveloping and very still. They dwarf the figures within them in an eerie way.

The human threat

Animals not only have to be wary of other animals, they are also under threat from human beings. Originally, hunting was essential for human survival: hunt for food or die. But once humans had started to raise animals (such as goats and chickens) for food, hunting took on a new purpose – it became a sport. Hunting scenes have been popular ever since as subjects for artists.

Eventually people added

▲ *Spots of bright red against dark green foliage remind us of drops of blood. Great white flowers add a shiver of fear. The steely embrace of the jaguar and the tangle of the horse's legs suggest rather than show the terrible act of slaughter. The horse merely looks surprised. How does the artist achieve this expression? Do you notice anything strange about the horse's legs?* [Horse Attacked by a Jaguar, *Henri Rousseau*]

money-making to their list of reasons for hunting. They began to kill animals for their fur or tusks to sell. In the 19th century, sailors risked their lives in small boats on whale-hunting expeditions. Whalemen carved the teeth and bones of the whales they caught with scenes of their terrifying battles with nature and the elements.

Gradually people became aware that whole species were in danger of being wiped out. They realized that animals needed protecting if they were to avoid extinction. Animal conservation societies were set up and many zoos, which before had been places of entertainment, took on new roles as centres for scientific research. In the last 50 years, some zoos have also become breeding centres for animal species in danger of extinction in the wild.

In spite of the recent awareness of the dangers of extinction, 20th-century technological advances mean that far more animals are killed now than ever before. Hunting expeditions that would once have taken months can now be achieved in a matter of days, thanks to cars and aeroplanes. This fact, and the fact that natural

▶ *This delicate and painstaking image of whaling is carved on a whale's tooth. It is a technique called scrimshaw. The seamen in these two small boats must have been terrified, as they would have been on every whaling trip, pitching their wits against the strength and fury of an animal fighting for its life. See how the whale tosses one of the boats into the air with a flash of its tail.*
[Scrimshaw of whaling boats from the east coast of North America]

Wildlife on TV

Since the 1950s, television wildlife documentaries have helped to increase our understanding of the natural world and the threats it faces. As film technology develops so do the possibilities for recording the most intimate moments in animals' lives. Sir David Attenborough's 'Life On Earth' series, first shown in 1979, made full use of the latest technology, including time-lapse photography and photography at 3000 frames per second. The series took more than three years to prepare, and involved the TV crew travelling more than one and a half million miles to over 30 countries.

The best wildlife programmes achieve high artistic standards and bring us close to an exciting, hidden world. Do you think George Stubbs would have enjoyed using a long-lens camera?

◀ *These two elephants are like mountains in motion. The threatening sky broods over the battle below. Look at the egrets flying in panic.* [Elephants Sparring, *Robert Bateman*]

Contact a wildlife organization and ask them to send you their information packs. What images do they use to convince you of their argument about animals under threat of extinction? How do these images work?

habitats are being reduced, means that many animals are under threat of extinction. The black rhino, the panda and the tiger are but a few of the animals that could disappear soon if nothing is done. Chemicals used in farming mean many small birds and butterflies are disappearing too.

Wildlife art

Nowadays wildlife conservation organizations commission artists to make images of animals under threat of extinction. These organizations hope that such images will not only teach people to respect wildlife but also to play an active part in the preservation of species.

Robert Bateman is an American artist known for his realistic wildlife paintings. At first glance they look as though they could be photographs (see opposite). But in fact each painting is the result of a long and painstaking process. Bateman's scientific knowledge is impressive. He makes numerous sketches, takes photographs for reference, sets up miniature landscapes with twigs and pebbles to enlarge into the finished work. He also uses a mirror – he finds that viewing the painting in reverse shows if the power and rhythm he is looking for is present in the painting.

Animals in motion

When Robert Bateman began trying to capture animals in motion, his teacher said: 'to learn to draw, you have to make 2000 mistakes – go ahead and make them'. You must be prepared to do the same. Be patient. Watch an animal closely for as long as you can. A TV wildlife programme will help.

What you need
- pencil
- paper
- video of a wildlife programme

What you do

1 Watch the film through several times.
2 Choose a moment you would like to capture.
3 Hit the pause button and start drawing quickly.
4 Wind back and pause as often as you need.
5 Don't rub out. As you add more lines, the animal may appear to move. Soon you will find you can sketch quickly and accurately with very few lines. You can add details of marking and texture later.

About the artists

(Only some of the artists are listed below. Many of the works of art in this book are by artists whose names we no longer know.)

AGASSE, Jacques-Laurent (1767-1849) This Swiss artist was born in Geneva. He was second only to Stubbs as the fashionable animal painter of his time. He worked in England most of his career, but he was a lonely man, always homesick for Switzerland.

AUDUBON, John James (1785-1851) This flamboyant American character always dressed as a woodsman and told exaggerated stories of his many adventures. The novelist Walter Scott was his hero.

BATEMAN, Robert (b. 1930) Lives on an island off the coast of British Columbia, Canada, but travels widely. He says he is 'hooked on nature, like some are hooked on computer games'.

BOTTICELLI, Sandro (1445-1510) This Italian artist was born in Florence. He was a superb draughtsman. Although he painted Greek mythical subjects such as *The Birth of Venus*, he was a devout Catholic and painted religious themes too.

CAILLEBOTTE, Gustave (1848-94) He was a French painter of French life. He collected paintings by other artists of his time.

CURRIER, Nathaniel (1813-1888) 'Printmaker to the American people'. He started work at the age of 15 and established his own business in The Grand Central Depot for Cheap and Popular Prints. He took J.M. Ives as his partner. The speed of his lithographic printing technique caused a sensation.

DÜRER, Albrecht (1471-1528) A German painter, engraver and designer of woodcuts. He travelled across Europe and made watercolours of scenes he passed. He liked to be seen as a fashionable 'man about town'.

GERICAULT, Théodore (1791-1824) A restless and romantic French painter, graphic artist and sculptor who died aged 33. He loved horse-riding and often raced horses.

HALL, Clifford (1904-1973) An English draughtsman, painter and illustrator. He painted clowns and the circus, suggesting the 'down side' of life in subtle ways.

HICKS, Edward (1776-1849) Born in the Delaware Valley near Philadelphia, USA, a farming community where he lived all his life. He was a deeply religious Quaker and self-taught artist who started out as a carriage painter.

IVES, James Merritt (1824-1895) Book-keeper to Nathaniel Currier, he rose to become his business partner and brother-in-law. He shared Currier's 'nose for news'.

LANDSEER, Sir Edwin (1803-73) British artist who was immensely popular as a painter of animals embodying human virtues – and vices! He designed the lions at the foot of Nelson's Column in Trafalgar Square, in London.

LEONARDO DA VINCI (1452-1519) Italian painter, sculptor, architect, mathematician, scientist, writer and musician. Few of his paintings survive, but many of his drawings of nature, the human form and designs for all sorts of gadgets, including flying machines, still exist.

MARC, Franz (1880-1916) A German artist who found animals more beautiful than 'ugly humans'. He tried to paint from the point of view of the animal, and find its essence. He was killed in World War I, aged 36.

MERIAN, Maria Sybille (1647-1717) Born in Switzerland but lived most of her life in

Holland, apart from a visit to Surinam in South America. She wrote and illustrated natural history, making an important contribution to art and science through her beautifully detailed illustrations.

MOLNÁR, C Pál (1894-1981) Hungarian book illustrator and painter of religious subjects, family scenes, street scenes and nudes. He explored abstract themes later in his career.

MUYBRIDGE, Eadweard (1830-1904) Known as 'father of the motion picture', Muybridge was born in England but lived and worked in the USA. A very colourful character, inventor and innovator, he changed his name from Edward because he felt the medieval spelling was more romantic. He was once tried for murder, but found not guilty.

POINT, Susan A. (b. 1952) Lives in Vancouver. She uses a silk screen technique for her prints, but also carves wood and designs glass engravings.

POTTER, Beatrix (1866-1943) Wrote and illustrated many well-loved children's books. She ran a sheep farm in the Lake District, the setting and inspiration for Peter Rabbit, Mrs Tiggywinkle and her other characters.

ROUSSEAU, Henri (1844-1910) This French painter was known as 'The Douanier', meaning 'customs officer', because that was his occupation. He taught himself to paint by copying paintings in the Louvre museum in Paris. He was immensely proud of his work and thought of himself and Picasso as the 'two great painters of the age'.

SADAHIDE, Utagawa (1807-1873) Lived and worked in Edo, now called Tokyo. His popular woodblock prints of *Pictures of the Floating World* were sometimes hand coloured.

STUBBS, George (1724-1806) English painter who made his experiments in Yorkshire and Lincolnshire. He did not like to be thought 'just an animal painter'. His portraits and 'conversation pieces' (figures arranged informally) are elegant mirrors of his age.

WOODROW, Bill (b. 1948) Lives and works in London. He uses ordinary bench tools – metal-shears, pliers, an electric drill – to create his sculpture. He uses whatever is to hand as his material – modern household equipment or discarded machines, for example.

Acknowledgements

Coast Salish Arts, 4; Bill Woodrow, 8; Private Collection, on loan to the National Gallery, London, 13; The Royal Collection © Her Majesty Queen Elizabeth II, 14; Peter Newark's Pictures, 18; Zefa, 20; From the collection at Parham Park, W Sussex, UK, 29; Philadelphia Museum of Art, bequest of Lisa Norris Elkins, 38; The Mariners' Museum, Newport News, VA, 43; Madison Press Books, 44.

All other pictures are from the Bridgeman Art Library, courtesy of the following: Musée des Beaux-Arts, Lille/Giraudon, 6; Private Collection, 10; Bonhams, London, 11; Victoria and Albert Museum, London, 12; Bibliothèque Nationale, Paris, 17; Anne Hall, 19; Galleria degli Uffizi, Florence, 23; British Museum, London, 24; Victoria and Albert Museum, London 25; Cheltenham Art Gallery and Museums, Gloucestershire, 27; Christie's, London, 28; Victoria and Albert Museum, London, 30; Christie's, London, 31; Stapleton Collection, 32; Fitzwilliam Museum, University of Cambridge, 33; Victoria and Albert Museum, London, 35; Dr Csillag Pálné/ Magyar Nemzeti Galeria, Budapest, 36; House of Masks, Delos, Greece, 37; Gallery 43, London, 41; Pushkin Museum, Moscow, 42.

Index